KIRKE MECHEM

FOR SOPRANO AND PIANO

Front cover artwork:
Fine Arts Museums of San Francisco,
Gift of Mr. and Mrs. John D. Rockefeller 3rd, 1993.35.20

ED 4012
First Printing: October 1997

ISBN 0-7935-6690-8

Associated Music Publishers, Inc.

DISTRIBUTED BY
HAL•LEONARD®
CORPORATION
7777 W. BLUEMOUND RD. P.O. BOX 13819 MILWAUKEE, WI 53213

PREFACE

To an Absent Love consists of three songs and an epilogue. The first, "Dear Husband," is an arrangement of an aria from my opera *John Brown*. The text is an actual letter written by a slave mother, Harriet Newby, to her husband, Dangerfield, one of Brown's raiders at Harpers Ferry. Dangerfield was killed in the raid; his wife was sold to a slave dealer in Louisiana.

No. 2, "A Farewell," is from my cantata, *The Winged Joy: A Woman's Love by Women Poets*. The poem is by Harriet Monroe (1860–1936).

The text of No. 3, "Fair Robin I Love," from my opera *Tartuffe*, is an adaptation of John Dryden's poem "Fair Iris I Love" (1690). In the opera it is an interpolated quotation, purporting to be an old folk song, sung by the saucy maid Dorine.

The Epilogue is an original song to a poem called "Debts" by the American poet Jessie B. Rittenhouse (1869–1948). It is the only one of the texts in which the "addressee" is not explicitly absent. I cannot say exactly why I chose to believe that the poet was looking back on a love that had ended or was about to end; I only know that these words seemed to call for music that was beautiful but somehow resigned and inexpressibly sad—as though the poet were writing a farewell letter, trying to end an ecstatic but impossible love.

— KIRKE MECHEM

I. Dear Husband

"Dear Husband:
Come this fall without fail.
I want to see you so much.
That is the one bright hope I have.
If you do not get me,
Somebody else will.
It is said that Master will sell me;
Then all my hopes will fade.
If I thought I should never see you again,
This earth would have no charms for me.
The baby has started to crawl.
The other children are well.
Oh that blessed hour
When I shall see you once more!
You must write me soon
And say when you can come."

II. A Farewell

Goodbye!—no, do not grieve that it is over,
    The perfect hour;
That the winged joy, sweet honey-loving rover,
    Flits from the flower.

Grieve not—it is the law. Love will be flying—
    Yes, love and all.
Glad was the living—blessed be the dying.
    Let the leaves fall.

III. Fair Robin I Love

Fair Robin I love and hourly die,
But not for a lip, nor a languishing eye;
He's fickle and false, and there we agree,
For I am as false and as fickle as he.

We neither believe what either can say;
And neither believing, we neither betray.
'Tis civil to swear and say things, of course;
We mean not the taking for better or worse.

When present we love; when absent agree:
I think not of Robin, nor Robin of me.
The legend of love no couple can find,
So easy to part or so easily joined.

IV. Epilogue ("Debts")

My debt to you, Beloved,
    Is one I cannot pay
In any coin of any realm
    On any reckoning day;

For where is he shall figure
    The debt, when all is said,
To one who makes you dream again
    When all the dreams were dead?

Or where is the appraiser
    Who shall the claim compute
Of one who makes you sing again
    When all the songs were mute?

To an Absent Love is also available in a version for
Soprano, Clarinet, Horn, and Piano, from the G. Schirmer rental library.

duration: ca. 13 minutes

for the Beaumont Ensemble:
Sara Ganz, Gregory Dufford, William Klingelhoffer, Joan Nagano

TO AN ABSENT LOVE

Text: letter from
Harriet Newby, a slave *

Kirke Mechem
Opus 58

I. Dear Husband

* See notes

II. A Farewell

Harriet Monroe*

Tranquillo, senza trascinando (♩ = ca. 60)

p espressivo, ma semplice

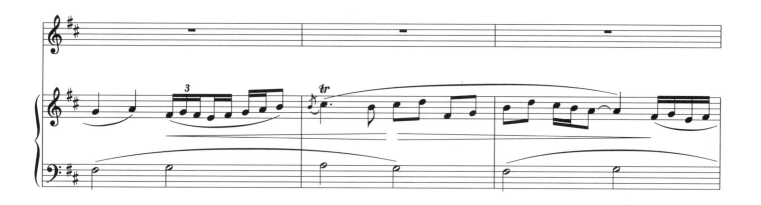

p espressivo, ma semplice

Good - bye! —— no,

do   not   grieve —— that it is   o - - ver,   The per - fect

* Used by permission of Houghton Mifflin Company, Boston

III. Fair Robin I Love

John Dryden
from *Amphitryon* (1690)

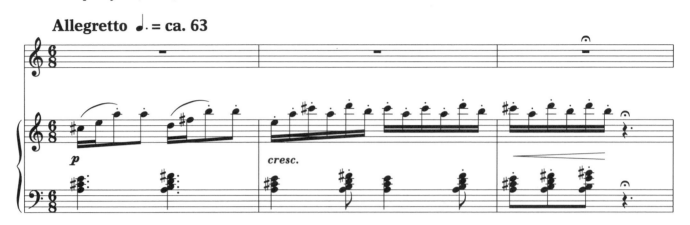

Fair Rob-in I love and hour-ly I die, But not for a lip, nor a

lan-guish-ing eye; He's fick-le and false, and

IV. Epilogue
("Debts")

Jessie B. Rittenhouse

Andante sostenuto

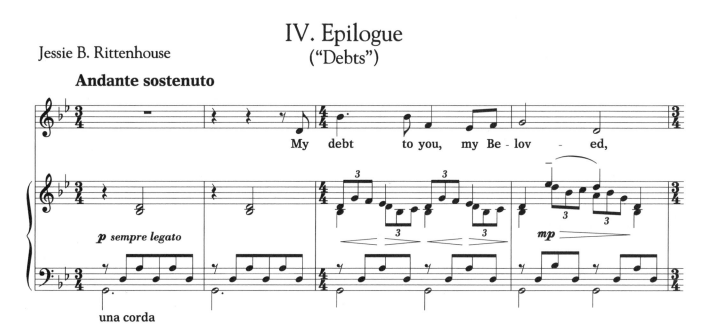

My debt to you, my Be - lov - ed,

p sempre legato

una corda

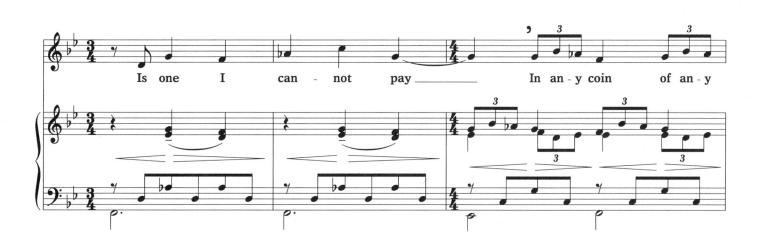

Is one I can - not pay In an - y coin of an - y

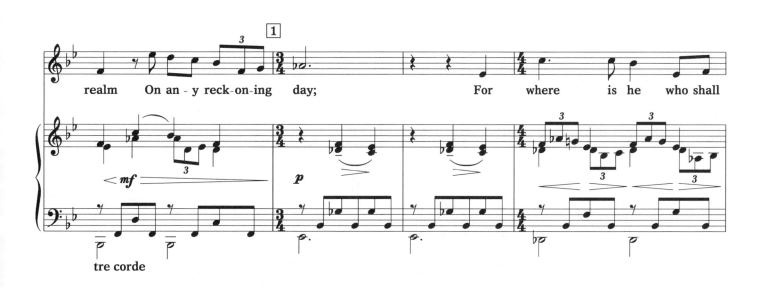

realm On an - y reck-on-ing day; For where is he who shall

mf *p*

tre corde

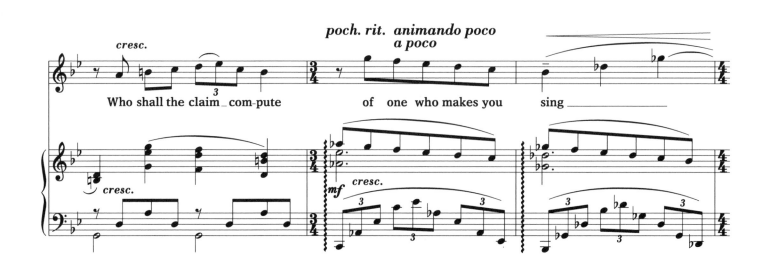

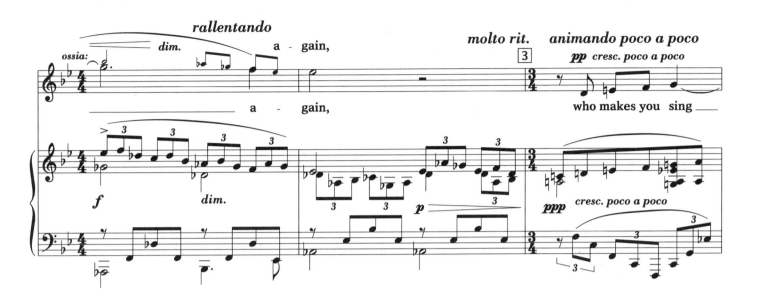